STRESS [

BOLD AND EASY COLORING BOOK

54 coloring pages,
featuring Bold and Easy Designs
for Adults, Teens and Kids.

PUBLISHED IN 2025 BY PAGE PUBLICATIONS

STRESS RELIEF
BOLD AND EASY COLORING BOOK

Place a piece of paper behind your
artwork to prevent bleed through.

this book belongs to

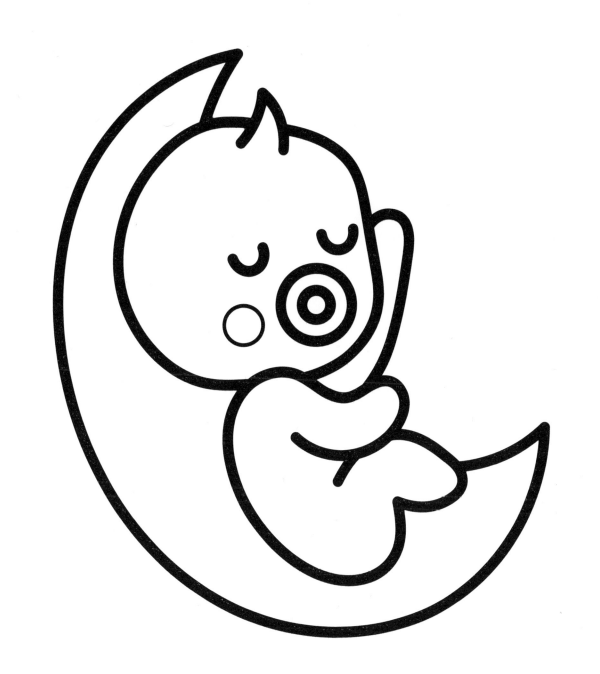